MOVEMENTS IN WORLD ART

EGYPTIAN PAINTING

MOVEMENTS IN WORLD ART

(edited by Heinrich Neumayer)

Heinrich Neumayer: EGYPTIAN PAINTING

Etta Becker-Donner: ANCIENT AMERICAN PAINTING

Roxane Cuvay: CAVE PAINTING

MOVEMENTS IN MODERN ART

Peter de Francia: IMPRESSIONISM

Denis Mathews: FAUVISM

Edith Hoffmann: EXPRESSIONISM

Alfred Schmeller: CUBISM

Alfred Schmeller: SURREALISM

Frederick Gore: ABSTRACT ART

HEINRICH NEUMAYER

EGYPTIAN PAINTING

Translated by Margaret Shenfield

WITH 24 COLOUR ILLUSTRATIONS

METHUEN & CO LTD
36 ESSEX STREET, LONDON WC2

EGYPTIAN PAINTING

The basic attitudes behind Egyptian art and the way in which these are expressed are the first things that must be considered here. The Nile, upon whose spring floods the year's food-supply depends, is the life-blood of the narrow fertile area. Whether the year will be lean or fat is determined by the Nile's drought-quenching waters. From the earliest times Egyptians have been preoccupied with a desire for permanent irrigation, for the river to overflow regularly. The coming of the Nile floods was the decisive event of the year, when life was reborn out of arid death, a fact which explains why Osiris became so firmly established as Egypt's most powerful deity — the mighty god who rose up from his grave, a symbol of the fate of the land. The rulers of Egypt, in their divinity, were primarily bringers of fertility, and afterwards governors of a realm whose frontiers were always being wiped out by water. Durability, unalterability, recurrence — these were the important values. And these values formed the basis of art. Perhaps sculpture was best able to express the essence of this inner desire. For thousands of years noteworthy sculpture was created in the Nile area. Differences in quality can be clearly seen as the art develops; there are bound to be climaxes and bouts of degeneracy over a period of thousands of years. But the large-scale sculpture of Egypt always remains calm, static, self-contained: it might be described as "sculptural" sculpture. Egyptian monumental sculpture uses only a few forms — the seated subject, imposing and calm, the squatting subject, and the equally calm standing subject. The standing subject extends one foot but his weight remains on the other, so that as the balance of the body is not shifted he does not turn into a walking figure but remains static.

One period after another remained substantially faithful to the traditional forms; the gifts of individual artists found expression in the quality of the execution, not in the creation of new forms. When Akhenaten introduced certain new artistic ideas and had himself portrayed not as a calm, monumental figure, but drawing his daughter towards himself with charming familiarity, this was as radical as his religious revolution (he tried to make the cult of the sun the only acknowledged religion). And the artistic revolution seemed to threaten the very foundations of the Egyptian desire for permanency in the agricultural pattern.

5

The development of Greek sculpture provides a direct contrast. The Greeks learned sculpture from the Egyptians; it came to them via the islands. A seafaring people, who enjoyed the unpredictability of an adventurous life (this is true of their most flexible tribes, at least), they soon loosened up the static sculpture that they learned. The arms were raised, the legs altered to suggest movement; it was not long before the static sculpture of the archaic period turned into the classical style of Olympia and the mobility of, say, Laocoon. Soon the Greeks were taking up bronze-casting, which the Egyptians used only for small commercial objects, and this made it possible to represent every kind of movement. For their large-scale sculpture the Egyptians preferred stone, and generally hard stone which suggested permanence. Not because they did not know of metal-casting, but because they made different demands on art — demands governed by spiritual laws and springing from the very centre of their nature. The hierarchy of the pharaonic empire, the sacred order with its greatness, endurance and tyranny must be borne in mind when we consider Egyptian art, just as the flexibility of the small city-states of Greece and the anthropomorphic quality of their gods must be borne in mind when dealing with Greek art. In Greece the gods turned into living human creatures; in Egypt the human rulers acquired the rigidity of divine mummies.

To the Egyptians, with this basic spiritual attitude, painting existed to stress the eternal, the permanent and the sacred. It is not merely because Egyptian painting now survives only in temples and tombs that its greatest achievements are thought to have been linked with such monuments; the Egyptians' tremendous preoccupation with gods and the next world make this inevitable. In the same way the powers of Christian art in the Middle Ages were lavished almost exclusively on places of worship. As a people the Egyptians were unusually fond of decoration. Not a wall of their (often huge) temples, not a wall of their numerous extensive tombs, remained bare. They were all covered with reliefs, paintings and writing. Although we are particularly concerned with painting, it is impossible not to treat the picture-writing, for the most part, as painting; in the same way, colour is such an essential component of Egyptian reliefs that they too must often be considered rather as painting than as sculpture. Nevertheless the painted scenes in the tombs are, of course, the characteristic works of ancient Egyptian painting. There is a whole cornucopia

6

of such paintings in the burial-grounds around ancient Thebes, the famous tombs in the Valley of the Kings and the Valley of the Queens, and the particularly delightful tombs of dignitaries who remained near their dead pharaohs even after death.

The ancient Egyptian painting still in existence, therefore, comes mainly from the tombs; if we include painted reliefs, then it comes also from the temples. The mummified corpses were entombed outside the flood area, in the desert. In the Old Kingdom the simple barrows began to be replaced (at least for corpses of high rank) by strong buildings on a rectangular plan and with sloping walls. These buildings were called mastabas, and the materials used were bricks or blocks of limestone. This simple structure was extended towards the east and a cult-chamber or chapel was added. By the fifth dynasty the mastaba contained a series of rooms. The best examples of these are to be found in the burial-ground of Saqqara, near ancient Memphis. The walls of these rooms were decorated with hieroglyphics and coloured reliefs. The mastabas of the great surrounded the king's tomb, then also a mastaba, although it later assumed the form of a step-pyramid, and later still a straight-sided pyramid. The royal tombs of the New Kingdom are different. As early as the Middle Kingdom high dignitaries had already begun to build their tombs into the rocks of the surrounding mountains. From the eighteenth dynasty onwards the pharaohs followed their example and built rock-tombs in the slopes of a solitary valley near Thebes on the west bank of the Nile. This "Valley of the Kings" contains numerous tombs which extend for varying distances into the rock. Long corridors lead to the rooms and the walls are often lavishly covered with paintings. This is the richest source of our knowledge about Egyptian painting. The tomb-temples stand on the plain between the Nile and the mountains; they have, of course, suffered greater damage. The rock-tombs of the pharaohs' wives are to be found in the Valley of the Queens and the finest nobles' graves in Sheikh Abd el-Kurna; these last, however, are more modest in design, although their paintings are often particularly charming. The tombs near Thebes date from the eighteenth, nineteenth and twentieth dynasties.

What are the subjects of the pictures in these tombs? The gods, religious ceremonies and scenes of life on earth; these are the most numerous and, owing to their graphic liveliness, the most attractive to us. According to the ceremonial scale of values we must begin with the pictures of gods.

7

In ancient Egypt religious beliefs were not codified in an ordered system valid for every region and every age. After, and alongside, fetish-worship, the worship of local gods with their special legends developed towards less primitive religious attitudes. The significance of the various regions and main towns within the overall pattern changed; the pharaohs' place of residence altered from period to period. For this reason alone the importance of various local gods was stressed at different times.

In connection with the painting illustrated in this book it is worth noting certain characteristics of god-worship during the period of the New Kingdom. The sun was commonly worshipped as a god in many regions; and different versions of the sun-god were blended together to form the god Ra, who also had several other distinguishing names. His symbol is the winged sun-disk. The journey of the sun through the hours of the night is told again and again in the tomb-paintings. The other deity worshipped all over Egypt was Osiris. Originally Osiris was a local fertility god. Around him grew up an extensive body of legends which, with their exciting and moving elements, gained wide currency. Osiris was a good ruler, a benevolent liberator, a bringer of civilization who was killed by wicked relatives. His sorrowing wife Isis discovered his corpse which was dismembered by Seth his brother, and had to be painfully put together again. The lamentation brought the dead Osiris back from the underworld. Because of his death and resurrection he became lord of the kingdom of the dead and a guarantee of the next life.

The moment of the dead man's arrival in the next world was of great importance for he had to stand trial immediately. Anubis led him to the judges, and he then had the opportunity of making a statement about his deeds on earth. According to the rules, the dead man enumerated all the occasions he had had for doing evil and stated that he had not taken advantage of them. Finally there was the test of truth. The dead man's heart was placed on one side of a pair of scales and a statuette of truth on the other. The dead man begged his heart not to testify against him. Anubis then looked carefully to see if the sides of the scales balanced one against the other. If he passed this test the dead man went on to the kingdom of Osiris and the fearsome monsters had to lie in wait for other victims.

Another point to be borne in mind is that Egyptian gods were often portrayed with animals' heads. Many animals were gods and were worshipped as such, particularly in the early period, but there were also gods with animal heads and, finally, animals which were associated with the gods. It is very striking to find a surviving burial shrine in Saqqara in whose huge rooms Apis gods — that is, bulls with particular markings — have been buried with all honours. In other places there are tombs for cats, ibises and crocodiles. Certain animals were associated with gods in human form. In the kingdom of the dead Anubis's animal was the dog, Horus's the hawk; cows, rams, ibises and other creatures went with various other deities. The close links between animals and anthropomorphic gods finally evolved into the concept of the animal-headed god. This recurs again and again in the paintings of gods.

The religious subjects in the tomb-paintings are mostly connected with burial. The carefully embalmed mummy of the noble corpse is shown being brought with great ceremony to the Nile, carried to the other (western) bank in a barge and placed in a rock tomb. The long, ceremonial procession is rather like a removal. Many objects for the next world, the whole contents of a house, accompany the corpse and are meant, no doubt, to be admired. A chorus of lamenting women proclaims the family's sorrow. In the tomb itself the priest performs the opening of the mouth, an important ceremony which enables the mummified, swaddled limbs to move again, and so fits the corpse for its new life. After the sorrowful farewell, the funeral meal takes place near the tomb; in this singers and harpists play an important part.

But to us the most appealing pictures are those showing daily life. They make up a great picture-book illustrating in rich and charming detail all the spheres of activity of the Egyptians. The tombs of the kings and nobles are decorated with paintings. It is their way of life which is portrayed; but since their way of life involves the lives of various other classes, these paintings teach us about more than one stratum of society. The royal tombs and the temples of the kings show official life, especially warfare and conquest, followed by scenes of the vanquished bringing tribute or captives in chains. The pharaohs are shown offering sacrifices to the gods, who receive them almost as equals. The paintings in the tombs of the nobles are more intimate and appealing. Not all Egypt shared the same concept of life after death. The only general belief was that death was not the end of life. If certain conditions were fulfilled, the dead man could go on living as though he were on earth. Consequently the body was carefully preserved; a house was built for the corpse and the tools and ornaments buried with him were to be of use in his new life. The things that could not be put in the tomb — a large retinue of servants, the pleasures of hunting and sailing — were painted on the walls as a substitute. These scenes tell us a great deal about the occupations and activities of the dead dignitaries. For example, the walls of one very famous mastaba at Saqqara mirror the life of the king's chief architect, Ti. He himself is portrayed, large and with the symbols of power, in a relief in the antechamber. Nearby the theme is his food; peasant women bring things to eat and there are pictures of their poultry-yard and of pigeons being fed. One wall shows the slaughtering and cutting up of the sacrificial animals; servants arrive with fish, and Ti and his wife watch the cranes being fed: in short the subject of food is well covered. Ti is also shown being carried on a litter, preceded by servants with fans; in other scenes he receives accounts from his subordinates and watches boats on the Nile coming in to land and herds being brought to him. As a magnificent diversion, he goes on a journey down the Nile and the boat glides through the papyrus thickets. Dancing-girls and singing-girls provide him with entertainment. He watches the harvest being brought in and six scenes show the reaping, transporting, threshing, sifting and packing of the corn. On another wall we can see — with our own eyes, as it were — ships being built for Ti, and the coloured relief shows us every detail from the cutting down of the tree-trunks and the moment when they are sawn into planks right up to the finished ship. The other craftsmen are equally industrious; there are pictures of carpenters, stone-masons and leather-workers. It is restful to turn from these to a banqueting scene, and the repeating sequence of farmers bringing taxes is even more soothing. But the greatest pleasure shown is the multiple hunt in the Nile delta which combines fishing, fowling and hippopotamus-hunting. The mural reliefs provide all this and more for Ti in his life after death.

As to the artistic significance of the art-forms, there has been some doubt as to whether and how far the painted reliefs should be considered as painting. The fact is that up to the New Kingdom, to about the period of the temple of Hatshepsut, reliefs were painted with ever-increasing care, so that the colour was a decisive characteristic and an equal partner in producing the artistic effect. Just as the sun lit up the year all over the country, so the Egyptians wished for colour to light up their architecture, sculpture and, above all, reliefs. Moreover Egyptian reliefs were low reliefs, often very flat, and indeed in many cases sunk reliefs. So it seems justifiable to consider certain examples of the art of relief as painting.

Egyptian wall-painting was done on the faces of limestone rocks, so that a painting-surface had to be created for the drawing and colour. At first painters took the trouble to make cavities in the stone in which a thick layer of paint could be laid on and rubbed in. Then — and this is the usual practice in the rock-tombs of the New Kingdom — they levelled up the rock-surface with clay and covered the whole with a thin layer of plaster. This provided a firm base for drawing and painting. But the amount of work done in the Ramesside period led to less care being taken. Painters hastily mixed any clay that was to hand with chopped straw, smoothed off the wall as well as they could and painted straight on to it. Even though much has survived, thanks to the exceptionally dry climate, these clay surfaces have suffered much damage since being exposed by those who discovered them. At first the Egyptians used reed-stems, splayed out at the end, as paint-brushes; later they used little brushes made of palm-fibre. Small bowls and shells were used to hold the colours. We know exactly what tools the painters (who were often only zealous craftsmen) used, and we know exactly how the painting was done, for very often the paintings were left uncompleted and the actual sequence of work can be observed. But before considering the use of colour, it is worth taking a look at the most immediately striking stylistic feature of Egyptian painting.

The figures and events shown in reliefs and paintings never stretch into the distance, but always remain on the surface. All foreshortening, every movement that would give depth, is avoided. The body is built up in the following way: the legs are in strict profile; the trunk is shown from the front, though this can represent any position depending upon the placing of the navel; the shoulders are seen from the front and the face in profile, although the eye is always frontal. The unnaturalness of this convention strikes one at the very first glance. However it is not at all disturbing, for we hardly consider naturalism a criterion — at least in decorative art. But one may well wonder how Egyptian art came to evolve this strict and unalterable rule. In our own times, in about 1900, various painters abandoned the realistic perspective which had been developed with such zeal and pride ever since the Renaissance. Architects, above all interior designers, had become sensitive to the fact that, by emphasising spatial qualities, the perspective in pictures destroyed space and created other rooms within the one large (real) room. The ancient Egyptians' feeling for space must have forbidden naturalistic perspective in much the same way. It was because of this that the rooms in the tombs took on the dignified calm, the monumentality and permanence that are, as was mentioned at the beginning of this introduction, the essential qualities of Egyptian art. They conform exactly to the laws of architecture and sculpture. There is also another point involved. The Egyptians were exceptionally devoted to narrative painting, and for it they used both writing and pictures, which indeed are identical in many cases. Moreover pictures were not only thought of as illustration but, in a magical way, as giving reality to the things depicted. Because of this magic and the narrative content it was important to show all the figures and circumstances with the greatest possible clarity; consequently the volumes were distributed as clearly as possible on the surface and all foreshortening was banished, since it clashed with direct exposition. Children who want their pictures to be explicit draw the figures with the same lack of artistic subtlety that the Egyptians raised to the status of a law. However we know that this convention stemmed from artistic convictions because there are certain calculated exceptions. In the interests of narrative clarity all the living creatures usually move along the wall in one direction; but when there is, for example, a statue among the living figures being taken to the tomb, its shoulders do not face forwards; its arm hangs from its flat profile chest. A table may be shown from the side, as a line only, or from above, as a rectangle; in pictures of many kinds of work the whole body has to be shown in profile. But for thousands of years the general rule remained unbroken, so that in this matter too Egyptian art is one of the most conservative of all time.

The scale of relative sizes in the paintings is well known and easy to understand; sizes vary according to rank. Pharaohs and gods are, obviously, entitled to loom above all others. The other figures vary in size from the great dignitaries to the lesser servants — each of whom still has a space to himself within the sequence — to the prisoners, who are usually painted in groups, packed close together and kneeling. It is chiefly on the pillars of the temples and in the tomb-chambers that the kings and gods can be shown on a great scale. Often god faces king with huge dignity; the ceremonies of greeting and sacrifice produce a monumental effect.

In the reliefs on the walls of the tombs the enlarged figures of the nobles appear in the narrative registers where they are forced to defend themselves as best they can against this reduction of their dignity. The reliefs and paintings in the rooms and corridors of the tombs make up long friezes running along the wall; they usually show events that are connected, such as agricultural processes, or the procession to the tomb; but they may also show unconnected episodes, such as hunting scenes or craft-processes. These registers are usually no more than about eighteen inches high. Each wall is generally devoted to a single theme. On the pillars are the life-size or larger pictures of kings and gods. When considering the friezes it is important to realize that their height is relatively modest.

The colours were provided by natural substances. Soot and ochre, and also powdered vitreous enamel (for blue and green) have been found in the paint pots. The paints were thinned with water and made to stick to the surface by means of a resinous gum. Ochre colours were used for the bodies of human beings and most animals; they show varying shades of red, brown and yellow. Women's bodies and faces are usually lighter than men's; often there are lighter and darker faces within a single female group, and lighter and darker bodies within a single group of men. Whitewash applied over reddish ochre produced the much-used pink. White alone was used for the clothes, and latterly also for the background. Different effects could be obtained by laying on different thicknesses of paint; a thin coat gave an impression of transparency. Hair was done in soot, a difficult medium which has suffered much damage. Blue and green were used for plants and decoration; they put considerable life into the pictures. Mixtures of these basic colours opened up further possibilities.

The scenes depicting the hoped-for life of the dead man in the New Kingdom tombs of the great show the Egyptian use of colour at its most delightful and subtle. The artist could let himself go, chromatically, when he was painting great heaps of fruit, or the banqueting-table or sacrificial altar, or fish in the net spread out in ornamental water, or noble ladies in costly jewellery enjoying a tactful conversation, passing each other fruit, sniffing at lotus blooms. The official state pictures of kings and gods gave opportunities only for a narrower range of traditional colours. Painters were called "makers of outlines" and there are indeed strong outlines in every painting, red or black lines which put a rigid limit round the figures; impressionistic haziness is unknown. How well the colours have survived depends on the natural substance used; soot was less lasting than chalk; the blue and green have altered with time, owing to their copper content. But the state of the colour also depends on locality. The dryness of the rock-tombs and the air of the region have preserved colours better than storage in a museum.

The most striking quality of Egyptian painting as a whole, the quality which should be stressed first, is its strong conventionality and the time its laws lasted. In the present age of rapid change in artistic aims it seems astonishing that an art could remain fixed in so many ways, for it demanded great discipline and restraint on the part of the artist. But this strict discipline is, like her fidelity to tradition, typical of Egypt. Like her most monumental architectural form, the pyramid, her graduated system of upper and lower ranks remained firm and unshakable. However, artists and craftsmen still had scope for individuality in presentation, although in many cases this was suppressed, so that the only differences are those of period. The rather stiff dignity, the careful but strict method of delineation, the narrow range of colours laid on thickly and clearly, all these lasted from the Old and Middle Kingdoms into the early part of the New Kingdom, to about the time of Tuthmosis III. From the middle of the fifteenth century B. C. the style became more individual, intimate and graceful. The background, blue before, became lighter, the colours more lively and, since more mixtures were used, more varied. Painting was most in demand in the Ramesside period, the twelfth century, when a great deal was painted that shows virtuosity but less care; the use of decoration is magnificent but there is nevertheless something rather commercial and tawdry about its prettiness.

A complete survey of Egyptian painting would include the papyri and, most important of all, the painting on the coffins, which have most attractive pictures of death-gods and tutelary gods on the insides of the lids. A later age, Egypt's Roman period, produced numerous mummy-portraits, particularly valuable historically but a form of painting which, in comparison with Egyptian art of the previous millenia, represents a falling-off, a lowering of the standard of religious painting, and an undoubted decrease in the now shattered monumentality of public art.

The plates in this book have been selected not for their fame or charm but to bring out the qualities of the art of the Pharaonic period.

14

BRIEF CHRONOLOGY

Old Kingdom	Dynasties III—VI	2778—2263 B. C.
Middle Kingdom	Dynasties XI—XIV	2133—1680 B. C.
New Kingdom	Dynasties XVIII—XX	1580—1085 B. C.

Dynasty XVIII: Ahmose I — Amenophis I — Tuthmosis I — Tuthmosis II Hatshepsut — Tuthmosis III (1504—1450) — Amenophis II — Tuthmosis IV Amenophis III — Akhenaten (Amenophis IV) — Semenekhkara — Tut-ankh-amon — Ay — Horemheb

Dynasties XIX—XX: The Ramessides

Greek Period: 332—30 B. C.

Roman Period: 30 B. C. — A. D. 395

PRINCIPAL SITES OF ANCIENT EGYPTIAN PAINTING

End of the Old Kingdom and beginning of the Middle Kingdom: the mastabas of Saqqara near Memphis.

New Kingdom: the temples and rock-tombs around Thebes: the Valley of the Kings, the Valley of the Queens, Deir el Bahari, Deir el Medina, Medinet Habu, Sheikh Abd el-Kurna.

BIBLIOGRAPHY

Aldred, C., *Development of Ancient Egyptian Art*, London, 1949—56

Capart, J., *Primitive Art in Egypt*, London, 1905

Davies N. M., *Picture Writing in Ancient Egypt*, Oxford, 1958

Mekhitarian, A., *Egyptian Painting*, London, 1954

Petrie, W. M. F., *Prehistoric Egypt*, London, 1920

Posener, G., *A Dictionary of Egyptian Civilization*, London, 1962

Rachewiltz, B. de, *Egyptian Art*, London, 1959

Sellman, R. R., *Ancient Egypt*, London, 1960

Smith, W. S., *A History of Egyptian Sculpture and Painting in the Old Kingdom*, Oxford, 1949

Vandier, J., *Egypt: Paintings from Tombs and Temples*, UNESCO, 1954

ACKNOWLEDGMENTS

Pl. 1—3, 5—24	Photo: Kurt Bachmayer, Vienna.
Pl. 4	Photo: Otto Tomann, Vienna.

15

Plate 1

CARPENTERS WORKING

Mastaba of Ti   Saqqara

The great burial ground of the Old Kingdom, that of Saqqara, is on a sandy plateau near ancient Memphis. "Mastaba" is the name given to those tombs composed of a burial-chamber at the bottom of a deep pit and other chambers rising above ground; the rectangular building which was all that could be seen was called after the Arabic *mastaba* ("bench"). Ti served two pharaohs as chief architect and superintendant of the pyramids. The reliefs on the walls of this mastaba are among the finest of the Old Kingdom; this plate shows a small section of the south wall of the burial-chamber. Higher up on the same wall Ti is portrayed three times on an impressive scale; near him are offering-bearers and game. His figure is four times larger than each of the narrative registers, such as these two from the lower part of the wall. Everything that comes within Ti's sphere of influence is provided, in pictures, for his use in the next world. In the upper register illustrated there is a particularly lively depiction of the carpentry trade. A man squatting on his haunches is sawing through a plank; next to him two standing figures are polishing a bedstead (a head-rest can clearly be seen under it); to their right is a man working with a drill. From pictures like these it is remarkably easy to reconstruct the daily life of the Nile area. The lower register shows goods being bartered. It is not composed as a whole but in small sections. In the upper register showing the four carpenters the grouping and use of line make the whole into a unified pictorial composition; in the lower one, on the other hand, each pair of figures is linked after the fashion of a metope. The colour aims only to make the bodies stand out, but it is so intense that the pictorial element nevertheless becomes a decisive factor. The walls of Ti's tomb are most informative; they also show shipbuilding and the entire range of farming, as well as the financial work of a government department.
According to the laws of style, the colour-reliefs of Egypt fall into the category of painting rather than sculpture.

Plate 2

PAYING TAXES

Mastaba of Ptah-hotep   Saqqara

The mastaba, or tomb, of Ptah-hotep dates from the fifth dynasty — the period from 2536 to 2423 B. C. when Egyptian civilization reached one of its peaks. The pyramid of one of the last kings of this dynasty, Onnos, is quite near the mastaba of Ptah-hotep, who was a high official. Its fine reliefs show, mainly, the worldly pleasures which will be available to the dead man in the next life. One of these pleasures is receiving the taxes due. This detail shows two men heavily loaded with natural produce which they are handing over. The first is leading an antelope on a rope; two birds hang from his arm by their wings, while with his other arm he carries a sheaf and a basket of fruit. The second man is grasping a bird in one hand, with which he also holds a rope attached to an antelope; his sheaf is stiff and straight, and three struggling birds are tied to his left arm. The sequence of tax-payers is continued on either side. The rigorous conventions of Egypt — the profile position of head and legs, the frontal position of the shoulders, etc. — are clearly recognizable in the manner of this painting. From the artistic point of view they represent the best way of decorating a low relief; from the psychological point of view they result from a desire to tell a story, to make the most striking impression possible.

The colour of the bodies (brick-red) and the hair (black) makes them stand out from the background, which is grey; the animals, skirts and sheaves are light-coloured.

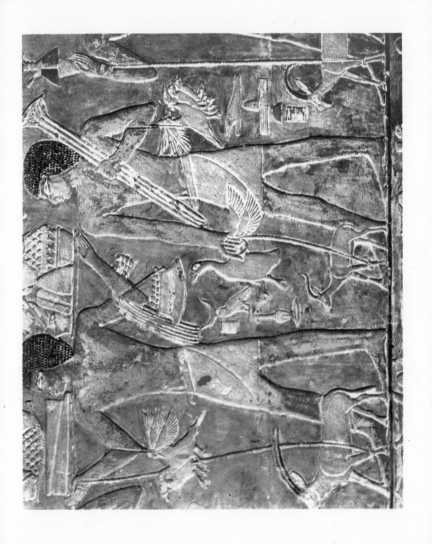

Plate 3

TUTHMOSIS III OFFERING A SACRIFICE

Temple of Hatshepsut   Deir el Bahari

The coloured reliefs in the temple of Hatshepsut, a huge building which took a long time to erect, are very well preserved and impressive. On one pier there is this depiction of King Tuthmosis making a sacrifice. The tall figure is very decoratively positioned on the wall-surface. His hands, with their long fingers, are holding the offering for the god — five spindle-like sticks, each having two feet and all standing on a tray. They represent an offering of cloth. Queen Nefertari is shown offering up cloth in the same symbolic way in her fine tomb. The slender figure in this painting probably originated as a portrait of Queen Hatshepsut, whose name Tuthmosis did his best to efface throughout the temple, often replacing it with his own. As a ruler Hatshepsut was always shown in male form, with the traditional beard, but the delicacy of the elegant figure, the obviously assumed beard, and the manner of making the sacrifice indicate that this is indeed Hatshepsut, even if her name has, as can be seen, been destroyed and the portrait assigned to Tuthmosis. The ceremonious dignity of the sovereign is well conveyed in this portrait. The figure of the deity being worshipped is only suggested; often gods too were erased if the worship of others superseded theirs. The red of the body and the yellow of the crown stand out strikingly against the background.

Plate 4

ANTECHAMBER OF THE CHAPEL OF ANUBIS

Temple of Hatshepsut   Deir el Bahari

Hatshepsut, daughter of the great Tuthmosis I, was married to her half-brother Tuthmosis II, who died early. From 1501 to 1480 she ruled as a female pharaoh. Then she married another and much younger half-brother, Tuthmosis III, whom she forced to remain in the background. As queen, Hatshepsut always had herself portrayed on her monuments wearing the royal beard and described as "Son of the Sun" and "Lord of Both Lands". It was she who had the huge and magnificent temple at Deir el Bahari built. When Tuthmosis III came to power he showed his hatred for Hatshepsut chiefly by having every mention of her name and every picture of her person erased. In the great temple he frequently substituted his own portrait for hers. Tuthmosis III became a great pharaoh, who built Egypt up into a powerful global empire, conquering Palestine, Phoenicia and parts of Syria. This illustration shows a portion of the temple. Polygonal columns support the antechamber shown, and the door leads to the Chapel of Anubis. The frame round the door and (at the very top) the frieze showing snakes, erect and guarding the sun, are of particular interest.

Plate 5

TUTHMOSIS III SACRIFICING TO THE GOD OF DEATH

Temple of Hatshepsut   Deir el Bahari

The huge temple-complex at Deir el Bahari is the work of Hatshepsut; when her brother and husband, Tuthmosis III, supplanted her, he added to the buildings. On the walls with decorations there are clearly recognizable erasures. The outstanding relief shown here is in the antechamber of the Chapel of Anubis. It shows Tuthmosis III offering up wine to the death-god, Sokaris. Sokaris was principally worshipped in Memphis, where he became identified with Osiris, and consequently converted into a god of death, whereas he had originally been an earth-god, a god of fertility. Tuthmosis is holding spherical vessels containing wine. He wears the crown of Lower Egypt, a broad neck-ornament, and an apron whose decorative girdle is bordered by the uraeus. The cartouches contain the names of Tuthmosis III, while on the left the reference to Hatshepsut has been deliberately and thoroughly wiped out. The broad-winged sun (surrounded by the uraeus) which is painted below the figures is very clear and formally beautiful.

Plate 6

ROYAL VULTURE AND FRIEZE OF SNAKES

Temple of Hatshepsut   Deir el Bahari

The antechamber of the Chapel of Anubis in the great temple of Hatshepsut is also the setting for this famous painting of the royal vulture and the frieze of snakes. The colours here are particularly well preserved. The vulture-goddess Muth holds a seal-ring in her talons; she is mistress of the starry heavens, which are indicated in a narrow strip above the divine bird and recur in a broader strip above the snakes. The ring is the symbol for "countless years", or eternity. The erect shield-bearing vipers have the red sun-disk on their heads; each disk is surrounded by cows' horns — the symbol of Hathor and of Isis. In places the symbols for life and endurance can also be seen between the suns. The vipers too carry the ring of "countless years". Tuthmosis III erased whatever was depicted below the vulture, so that it must have had something to do with Hatshepsut. Snakes protected the sun from enemies and also symbolized the crown of Lower Egypt. The fiery breath of the shield-bearing viper also protected the pharaoh. In its ornamental use of the motifs, the carefully executed borders and deep symbolism, this work is typical of the finest achievements of Egyptian painting.

E 26

Plate 7

SANDSTONE CHAPEL OF TUTHMOSIS III

Tuthmosis III was a mighty ruler who laid the foundations of a world empire. In about 1500 B. C., in fact, the far-flung Pharaonic empire developed into the great New Kingdom, which achieved enormous power and wealth in every sphere. The wealth is evident in the decorations and contents of this pharaoh's buildings; he undertook more ambitious projects than any of Egypt's other rulers. The coffin-chamber of his tomb in the Valley of the Kings, with its long, oval shape and rounded ends, imitates the shape of the name-cartouches of the pharaohs. The walls are covered with inscriptions in hieroglyphics, written in black or red on the wall, which is coloured yellowish-grey, so that the chamber gives the effect of a huge, encircling, and ornamental papyrus. The walls of the sandstone chapel (now transferred to the Cairo museum) are also covered with these ceremonial and sacred hieroglyphics. Two royal cartouches stand out in this detail. The left-hand one refers to the great Tuthmosis, the right-hand one to Amenophis II, his son. Within the frame "Tuthmosis" is made up of the following signs: at the top an ibis, the symbol of the ibis-god Thoth — which gives Tuth; beneath it the tripartite sign for "ms", and at the bottom the final "s" sign. This completes the name, since the vowels were not understood.

The tutelary vulture-goddess, Muth, mistress of the starry heavens, which form an ornamental band at the top of the wall, is shown in the customary manner holding the ring, the symbol of "countless years", or eternity. Below her is the symbol for life which occurs so often in paintings and which, in this context, can only refer to life in the next world. The whole wall is like one enormous, beautifully coloured design. It shows not only a fine sense of form but also a gift for symbolical abstraction, in the way that the royal names are stressed as the essential items and surrounded by every kind of magical protection. The good positioning of the symbols and the sparing colour give a strong impression of royal dignity. This mixture of symbols and pictures in coloured low relief belongs essentially to the province of painting; to the modern eye it looks rather like book-illumination on a monumental scale.

Plate 8

SETHOS BEFORE OSIRIS

Tomb of Sethos I   Valley of the Kings

In the antechamber which is numbered IX, one of the many rooms in Sethos I's long tomb, there are scenes showing the pharaoh facing the gods of death — Osiris, Isis, Hathor and Anubis. The king is, so to speak, making his first visits in the underworld. Sethos was an important ruler who drove off the Hittites. In this picture he confronts Osiris with great dignity. He wears the crown of Lower Egypt, from which a snake juts out, rich jewellery on his neck and arms, and a particularly fine piece of decoration on his loin-cloth. Osiris is always shown tightly swaddled, like a mummy, in a robe which reaches up to his neck. In his hands he holds a sceptre and a whip, the attributes of authority. On his head is his tall white crown, decorated with two feathers. His long thin beard is also characteristic. The cult of Osiris, whose legend became elaborate and extensive, spread from Lower Egypt into the whole country. Above the pharaoh are the two name-cartouches of Sethos I. To the left of the god is a column of symbols, the topmost of which are the symbol for life and the tower-like symbol of Osiris himself. The figure of the king is executed with great care.

Plate 9

RETINUE

Tomb of Sethos I

Valley of the Kings

The reliefs in Sethos I's tomb are well preserved and the long building contains fourteen rooms. The pictures show the pharaoh confronting various deities and their main subject is the nocturnal journey of the sun through the Kingdom of the Dead. Each separate hour of the night can be recognized in these scenes; they stick closely to the "book of him who is in the underworld". This detail shows a sequence of men who belong to the king's retinue. They form an interlude of ceremonial tranquillity amid the tumultuous waves of symbols above and below them. Each of the men has a single symbol by his left hand, which is no doubt intended to indicate his profession; otherwise the figures are uniform. The first man on the right is shown with the symbol for a house — a rectangle with a single small opening which represents the ground-plan. He is, probably, the superintendant of the house. The third man is probably an astronomer, and the fourth is shown with three sticks near his hand; when joined by a bow these signify "diadem". The bow is not visible, but if it were there the sign would indicate that the man was a treasurer. The procession-like arrangement of the men gives a feeling of calm dignity and an impression of large numbers. Although the painter may not be a great artist, his knowledge of tradition enables him to produce a striking effect.

Plate 10

THE PHARAOH BEFORE OSIRIS

Tomb of Amenophis II   Valley of the Kings

In the mastabas of the Old Kingdom pictures of daily life take up the greatest space — in other words, life in this world pursues the dead man; in the rock-tombs of the New Kingdom, on the other hand, the religious element is more heavily stressed. The kings are shown appearing before the deities after death. They usually bear a gift in their hands, but are almost the equals of the gods, whom they often represented in life on earth. This illustration shows the meeting of two figures who are almost equals; Amenophis is appearing before Osiris. Osiris is the royal god; his legend refers to a great king of remote antiquity. From his tomb he exerts a beneficent influence; he is responsible for the great flood which brings life to Egypt. As a god of death Osiris is shown in mummy-like swaddling. He wears the tall white crown of Upper Egypt and holds the crozier and scourge which symbolize the supreme power of command; and at this encounter he also carries another long staff, the sceptre crowned by the symbol of life which he is pointing towards the dead king. This is a simple way of expressing the god's grace towards the king. Amenophis wears the headdress of the pharaohs and the divine beard; on his forehead the uraeus rears up erect. This cobra, erect and ready for battle, is intended to protect the king from all his enemies, and the same tutelary deity is shown on the king's apron. The cartouche over his head proclaims his name.

The strongly emphasised outlines give this mural a highly graphic character. The thinner figure, the god, is shown entirely in profile and standing on a pedestal, so that he is raised to a more dignified height. The pharaoh is honoured with his natural stature and his customary frontal-profile pose makes a good contrast with that of the god. A formally beautiful border holds together the composition, which consequently seems more unified than is usual in Egyptian painting. The whole is splendidly well preserved; it is on one of the six pillars in the great hall of the pharaoh's tomb which leads into the burial-chamber itself.

Plate 11

MUSICIANS

Tomb of Nakht

Sheikh Abd el-Kurna (Thebes)

Nakht was a high dignitary of the eighteenth dynasty. One of the rooms in his tomb is decorated with particularly beautiful paintings. In one sequence Nakht is shown watching work in the fields; another reproduces the pleasures of harpooning and fowling. The register from which this detail is taken illustrates the pleasures of the banqueting-hall. Nakht is sitting at table with his wife; a servant is bringing geese and flowers, while musicians (as shown in this detail) play background music. The first girl is performing on a double flute, the second carries a lute with a strikingly long fret-board, and the third is a harpist. The girls' hands are particularly finely drawn; the whole composition of the group of three is outstanding. No doubt the nude is also a dancer; the curves of her turned head and bent leg start up a rhythm which is resolved in the heavy harp. On the other hand, the two clothed girls produce a more static effect; their hands make a horizontal link between the more agitated lines. The cones on their heads are generally considered to be ointment-holders, meant either to symbolize the sweet scent given off or, realistically, to show that such cones really held perfumed ointment. The painting tells us a great deal about the music-making of Egypt; artistically, it shows great skill in group-composition.

Plate 12

BANQUET

Tomb of Nakht   Sheikh Abd el-Kurna (Thebes)

The colours of the paintings in Nakht's small tomb are well preserved. One wall shows Nakht officiating in the fields; another shows him enjoying a banquet. Girls playing instruments are near him. The upper register of the picture of the banquet shows guests — seated ladies — and in front of them the famous blind harpist. The ladies wear close-fitting dresses and ornaments round their necks and on their heads. Immediately behind the musician a lady sits listening and smelling a lotus flower; the two ladies behind her are discussing the salve-pots or fruit which they are holding in their hands. A similar object is being passed to the lady whose hand is visible. Between her and her neighbour stands a very young girl who is nude like a dancer. On the ladies' heads are the ointment-holders which are one of the features characteristic of such parties. Even the harpist has one on his shaven head. He is shown seated, in strict profile, with the sole of one foot turned towards the spectator; bulges indicate that he is corpulent; his hands are plucking at the strings of a short harp. In antiquity singers were often portrayed as blind, probably as a result of the feeling that, in their poetry and songs, they concentrated on the sights and sounds within themselves. The great artist who painted this work succeeded wonderfully with the tragic expression of the harpist's face; the contrast between the ladies, who are enjoying themselves, and the depression of the musician also testifies to the artist's sensitivity. The colouring is delicate and shows great skill.

Plate 13

SURVEYORS

Tomb of Menna   Sheikh Abd el-Kurna (Thebes)

This painting on a wall of the tomb of Menna, Amon's "superintendant of the fields", captures an important scene in the life of Egyptian farmers: the surveyor assessing the harvest for tax purposes. For the farmers much depended on this. When the corn was ripe the surveyor came, bringing with him scribes and servants. In this painting he is shown holding the tool of his trade, a long rope with knots in it; no doubt the boy whose head reaches only to the top of the corn assists him with the surveying. A servant is holding the staff of authority. On the right a man is holding out a bag of corn whose quality is to be assessed, but it is probably also a symbolic gift to greet the awesome assessor; the man bringing it may well be the farmer. Behind him a woman is carrying a basket on her head and a heaped dish on the palm of her hand. These may be gifts to welcome the visitor or, possibly, measures from which the harvest will be estimated. The farmer holds an interesting object in his other hand; it may perhaps symbolize a corn-silo, for in Egypt these were conical in shape. The colouring of this painting stresses the red of the bodies, the yellow of the ripe corn and the white of the clothing; the background is fairly light.

Plate 14

STILL-LIFE

Tomb of Menna

Sheikh Abd el-Kurna (Thebes)

The tombs of Sheikh Abd el-Kurna belong to the high dignitaries of the eighteenth dynasty. Menna was Amon's minister of agriculture and land-surveyor. His work lives on in the paintings in his tomb, which are particularly graphic depictions of it; this illustration shows one example. The measuring and working of the fields should bear fruit, and this detail shows natural produce in a still-life composition of the finest, most delicate order. It produces the same impression as certain pictures of the present day by painters such as Matisse and Dufy. It is impossible to identify all the components of this sacrificial pile, but there are baskets, stylized figs, a bunch of flowers, a large fish which stands out, a goose with bent neck, bunches of grapes which provide dark accents. The comparative sizes seem arbitrary, but the linear structure of the whole is masterly. The colour is stronger at the base and gradually becomes more delicate as the pile rises, until the baskets at the top once again provide strong contours. This detail comes from a sequence which shows Menna receiving produce from fields and gardens; on the right we can see a hand pointing towards this mountain of rich offerings. In this frieze there are several charming pictures of animals and still-life — lightly stylized, very delicate in colouring, and painted by a master of decorative art.

Plate 15

CEILING DECORATED WITH STARS

Tomb of Menna   Sheikh Abd el-Kurna (Thebes)

The ceiling of one of the rooms in Menna's tomb is covered with decorative painting. It is fascinating to see the Egyptians, for once, tackling a project in purely ornamental terms. Between the restless zigzag bands there are stars. They are decorative but at the same time represent the image of a next world which did not always take the same form in Egyptian thinking. The hereafter was variously conceived as life on an island of blessedness, as a continuation of earthly joys, and also as more modest forms of existence. One of these conceptions assigned to the dead a place among the stars. There they shone out, threatened by many demonic constellations. At a later period the Egyptians' knowledge about the stars enabled them to read horoscopes. They felt that life was closely bound up with the stars from birth until entry into the next world. So it is understandable that stars should be painted on the ceiling of a tomb-chamber. In general it was rare for Egyptian artists to curb their love for story-telling, narrative painting. Here, however, the constellations are not conjured up and realized in paint; the star-form is shown for its own sake, stretching on into infinity. The yellow, or gold, of the stars is the colour most stressed.

Plate 16

FUNERAL

Tomb of Ramose   Sheikh Abd el-Kurna (Thebes)

Ramose was the highest official during the end of Amenophis III's reign and the beginning of Akhenaten's. His tomb is decorated with many paintings on stucco which are interesting from a historical, as well as an artistic, point of view. The south wall shows the funeral of the great lord; the choir of lamenting women, stretching out their hands, is very moving. This detail shows the objects which are to accompany the corpse being borne to the grave. On the left two servants are carrying the bed with its head-rest; the space between the two figures is bridged by a feather fan and some writing. The first servant also holds a multicoloured bag. He is preceded by a close group of four bearers carrying chests on their heads; the fourth man also has a staff, and the first a pair of elegant sandals which he is holding sole to sole. He is shown with two arms, whereas the second arm of each of the middle servants is hidden. The next figures are more spread out again; the second servant from the right carries a well-shaped chair and a writing-tablet while the man in front of him has some ointment-pots. The painter of this scene is too much of an artist to make the procession uniform; with great delicacy he separates single figures from groups, and red and yellow ochre distinguish the figures chromatically. The register above this one shows the procession of the coffin; the detail shown here adjoins the scene with the weeping women. The manner of this painting suggests a painter with a turn for elegance, who thought out his composition carefully.

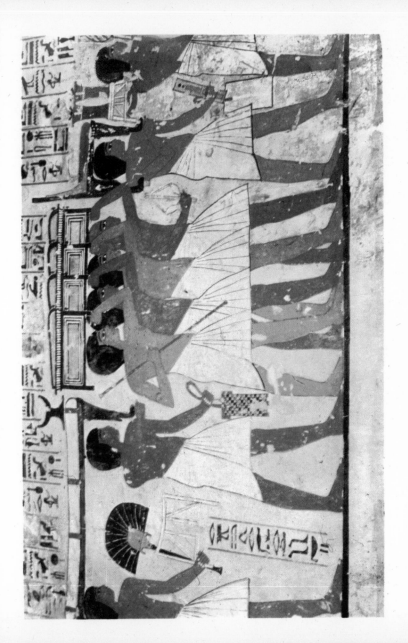

Plate 17

THE MOUTH-OPENING CEREMONY

Tomb of Tut-ankh-amon   Valley of the Kings

The discovery of Tut-ankh-amon's tomb in 1922 was a most exciting event. This pharaoh was Akhenaten's successor and the husband of one of his daughters. He died young; his mummy is that of an eighteen-year-old boy. The enormous riches of the coffins and accompanying objects are well known, as is the high level of artistry they display. The painting in the burial-chamber is much less skilful. The scene shown here is of interest since it portrays a religious ceremony. Tut-ankh-amon is depicted as Osiris; before him stands his successor King Ay, dressed as a priest and preparing to touch the dead man's mouth with a tool that often appears in paintings; it has a metal square inserted in the front portion. This mouth-opening ceremony was divided into several parts. Its purpose was to give the dead man back the use of his organs so that he could begin a new life in the next world. It was associated with anointing, which is indicated by the pots on the small table between the dead pharaoh and his living successor. The figure on the far left is holding the symbol of life which is appropriate to this ceremony.

Plate 18

WINGED SUN-DISK

Temple of Ramesses III   Medinet Habu

The door-lintel shown here comes from the magnificent temple of Ramesses III. Divided into two sections, it combines pictures and writing in a particularly successful way. The upper portion is filled by the winged sun-disk, a traditional form which recurs frequently. This is, therefore, an official picture. The writing below calls the disk "that of Edfu, the great god, the god of gay plumage, who goes out from the land of light, the lord of the sky". The two wings are the guardians of the two Egypts, Upper and Lower. They were an obvious symbol of imperial unity, like the double crown. Below, between the two cartouches bearing Ramesses III's name are the symbols for son, sun, life and god, side by side. The colours are really intense and, being well-preserved, they make this lintel, with its outstanding ornamental use of space, a noteworthy example of the great artistry of Ramesses III's reign.

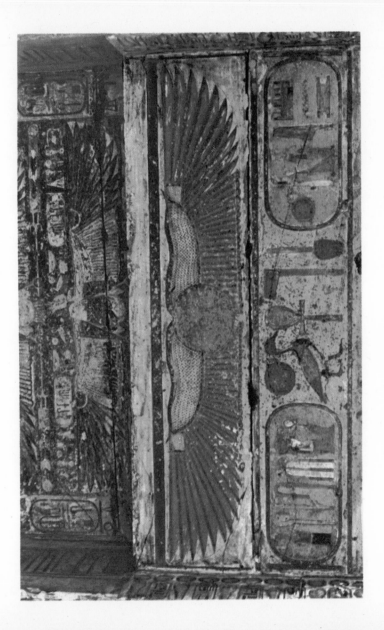

Plate 19

JOURNEY OF THE SUN

Tomb of Ramesses VI   Valley of the Kings

The dead in their tombs yearned for light. Their happiest hours came in the night when the boat of the sun came down and carried out its night journey. Light then shone out in the underworld. This journey was described in full detail in the sacred writings; the divisions and positions of the twelve hours were particularly carefully described and differentiated. In the tomb of Ramesses VI there are numerous pictures of the sun's journey through the underworld according to the text of the "Book of Gates". In the New Kingdom it was almost universal for the sun's night journey to be depicted on the walls of the kings' tombs. According to the sacred book, one of the gates was guarded by a fearsome snake which in this painting is shown arched over the gate in a series of powerful curves. This is the fourth part of the journey through the underworld; the snake, Teke-hor, must let the boat through. The sun-god is actually standing in the gate. He wears the ram's head which belongs to the journey through the underworld; in his right hand he holds the magic symbol of life, in his left the staff of authority. Apart from the god there are only two men on the boat, which is being drawn along by other men. The oars on the far left and the huge curves of the snake produce an effect of great dignity and simplicity.

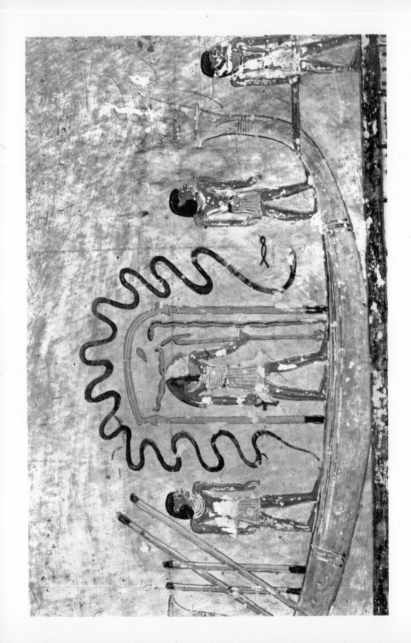

Plate 20

SCARAB

Tomb of Ramesses VI   Valley of the Kings

The Egyptians described the dung-beetle, or sacred scarab, as "that which lives" or
"that which begets itself". They believed that it was born out of the earth without
being procreated. The female of this dung-beetle, known as the "pillmonger", makes
a ball out of bits of dung and rolls it into a hole prepared in advance, which she then
covers over. Thus the eggs, when hatched, are warm, safe, and near food. But the
Egyptians thought that all scarabs were male and that each ball was an egg out of which
the beetle who laid it was reborn — just as the soul was released from the mummy.
The beetle with its ball became a symbol of the setting and rising sun, and a stone
scarab became a favourite amulet. It appears again and again on the walls of tombs —
the symbol of resurrection. Small stones were carved into miniature representations
of it; but it was often also represented on a colossal scale; the best known of these works
is that at Karnak. This painting, from the tomb of Ramesses VI, is interesting because
of the subject it illustrates. According to the religious beliefs of the Heliopolitans the
scarab was a sun-god who rose up to heaven. Here the beetle is shown breaking out
of the sun-ball and himself holding his ball, another small sun. He is portrayed with
wings, the attributes of the sun-god, as a token of his supremacy.

Plate 21

SUN-BARGE

Tomb of Ramesses IX   Valley of the Kings

While in Saqqara the reliefs surround the dead with all the rich life of this world, the New Kingdom tombs in the Valley of the Kings contain many more pictures of the night. The one which recurs most frequently is the journey of the sun through the hours of the next. The dead looked forward to the sun's journey through the "land of life", as the Egyptians euphemistically called the land of the dead. The sun could call on two barges. It used one in the morning, to travel across the sky; the barge "of the descent" was for the night journey. The evening sun-god is shown with a ram's head He had to pass through various gates and the hours were identified with great exactitude: this picture shows his position at the second hour of the night. In front of the sun-god stands Hathor, a kindly goddess whom the Thebans worshipped as the tutelary goddess of the city of the dead. Her sacred animal is the cow; hence her head is decorated with horns. In the god's retinue there are creatures with hawks' heads which indicate that they belong to the hawk-headed sun-god Horus, although for the moment he has assumed a ram's head. Even the oars are crowned with hawks' heads; the uraeus rears up from the prow. The wave-motif which borders the picture at the top and bottom alludes to the river journey. The many hieroglyphics tell of this episode of the journey. The paintings in the larger tombs of Sethos I depict nearly all the hours of the night journey. The colours have been applied with great care.

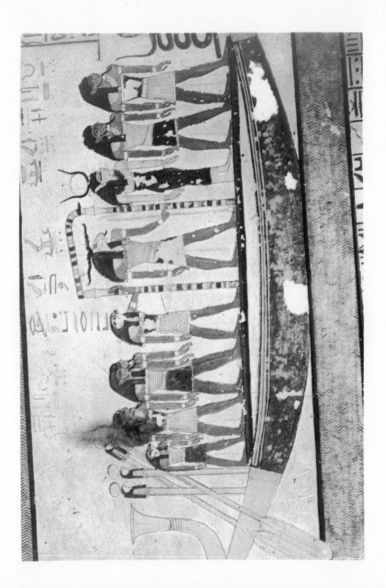

Plate 22

ROYAL CARTOUCHE

Tomb of Ramesses IX   Valley of the Kings

To our eyes the ancient Egyptians seem to have been fonder of writing than any other people the world has ever known. Wherever there was a free surface they covered it with signs. The walls of the tombs tell of the dead, and words accompany the scenes both in this world and in the next. For example they explain all about the sun's journey so that the dead man will be able to remember, and take advantage of, every opportunity. Naturally enough the name of the dead king appears again and again. Even at a casual glance it is impossible to miss the long oval shapes — rectangles with rounded ends — of the cartouches which, like coats-of-arms, contain the sacred signs appropriate to the king's name. The kings generally have two names, each of which has its own cartouche, although the two cartouches are placed close together. This is true of Ramesses IX who dates from the twentieth dynasty. The symbols in the first cartouche, which is illustrated here, give his official title. At the top is the symbol of the sun-god Ra, which as a sign also signifies the name Ramesses but is used here in its old form as a logogram and conveys that Ra has chosen Ramesses. This is supported by the bottom sign, a rake with a metal blade actually being used on the earth; this is the sign for "to choose". It is remarkable that the old logograms still linger on in the royal cartouches until quite late; being well composed and well disposed in the space they produce a fine pictorial effect. The colours used in this painting are yellow, red and black.

Plate 23

ANUBIS AND THE CORPSE OF OSIRIS

Tomb of Sennutem   Deir el Medina

In the gorge of Deir el Medina there are tombs dating from the period of the twentieth dynasty (1200—1090 B. C.). The tomb of Sennutem, an overseer of the necropolis, has a specially large number of well-preserved paintings. This plate shows an important scene from the legend of the god of death, Osiris. Seth, Osiris's wicked brother, had killed Osiris out of envy. Isis, his wife, found the corpse, but Seth was still angry and dismembered it. There are, however, frequent and important accounts of the resuscitation of the murdered god; this is certainly bound up with the belief in the rebirth of the fertile year under the protection of the god. This resuscitation was ascribed to various gods, but especially Anubis, who had a jackal's head. For it was Anubis who embalmed Osiris's corpse and thus sanctified it. In this plate we see Anubis at work on the god's corpse; the embalming seems to be finished and the resuscitation about to occur. In the mastaba period Anubis was still the death-god in the form of a jackal who prowled around the domain of the dead; the jackal, an animal that feeds on carrion was, in fact, appointed guardian of the dead. In Saqqara it is shown again and again in this capacity. Then Osiris took over this task, combining within himself, as he did, all beneficent gifts. As "Lord of the Divine Hall", Anubis was patron of the embalming ritual; he was the patron, too, of the guild of embalmers, a guild with a strict hierarchy of functions. As embalmer-god he had under his protection a ritual which could take seventy days when a king was the subject. The Taricheutes, or high-ranking embalmers, were counted as priests; when at work they wore dog-masks to make themselves look like Anubis.

The form of the painting illustrated is well balanced and its use of line is carefully thought out. The splendid bed and the god's corpse stand out sharply against the light background; Anubis's dark, canine body reaches up to the curtain-like decoration at the top and so loses height. This is an example of the good painting of the late period; the care it shows was soon to disappear from Egyptian art.

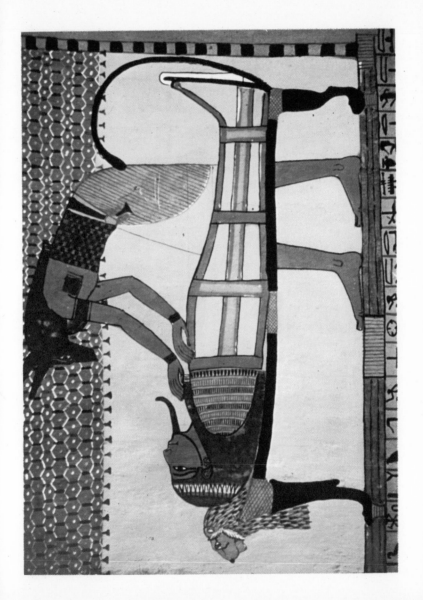

Plate 24

WORK IN THE FIELDS

Tomb of Sennutem   Deir el Medina

The east wall of the tomb built for Sennutem shows the Egyptian paradise floating on the sea, the Fields of Yaru, where palms grow and beautiful flowers bloom. In order to live there the dead man and his wife must share in the work of cultivation. Sennutem is shown ploughing, sowing, and reaping the corn. In this plate husband and wife are hard at work gathering in the flax. After working they will be qualified to kneel down before the gods on the sacred island. In the tomb space is limited and none of the episodes are depicted with any great artistry; but the scenes show sincerity and a fondness for narration. And even here the artist is clearly skilled in composition. In this detail there is a very successful crescendo of line from the clothed figure of the woman to the semi-clothed, taller figure of the man. The curves of the bodies and the flax have a simple and decorative effect. These paintings date from the twentieth dynasty when the quality of Egyptian art was already deteriorating. It is easy to compare the quality of earlier and later work by referring to the magnificent depictions of similar scenes in, for example, Saqqara.